Have You Seen a Self-Driving Car?

By
Elaina Ashton
Anna Prakash-Ashton Ph.D.

Illustrated by
Chad Thompson

Just Empower LLC
https://just-empower.com
Email: info@just-empower.com

Ordering Information: Quantity sales. Special discounts are available on quantity purchases by corporations, associations, and others. For details, contact the publisher at the address above.

ISBN (paperback): 978-0-578-66451-4
ISBN (ebook): 978-0-578-67131-4

Dedicated to my family

A portion of all proceeds supports our nonprofit,
Education Empowers Inc. (www.educationempowers.org)

Table of Contents

Have You Seen a Self-Driving Car?

Have you seen a self-driving car in your neighborhood?
Without a human driver, how do these self-driving cars see the road?
How do they see the environment around them?

Self-driving cars have eyes and ears. They are called sensors!

What are self-driving cars? A car with many eyes and ears? Think about it: it would be a lot harder to walk around safely if you couldn't see or hear! You have eyes and ears to help you get around. Self-driving cars have eyes and ears also. They are called sensors. Sensors are small machines that allow the car to look around and collect information. Self-driving cars are capable of driving themselves and don't need human drivers. They are sometimes called "autonomous" or "driverless" robotic vehicles.

Self-driving cars use sensors, cameras and computer vision software to detect objects around them and their distance.

GPS

LiDAR

Rear Camera

Video Camera

Radar

Ultrasonic Sensors

Odometry Sensors

Central Computer

Radar

How do self-driving cars work?
Self-driving cars use a number of cameras, sensors, and computer vision software to see objects, people, animals, obstacles, traffic lights, signs, and even the lines painted on the roads. All the information from the cameras, sensors, GPS, and INS goes to a computer which creates a 3D map. Using the map, the computer can decide which way to drive, when to brake or go faster, and how to steer. A self-driving car must gather a lot of information in order to get where it's going and keep its passengers safe!

More than a million people in the world die each year due to traffic accidents. Self-driving cars can make driving safer.

Can self-driving cars save lives?

Car accidents kill and injure many people. The NHTSA, a government agency that watches and records traffic issues, tells us that over 90% of vehicle crashes are caused by human error, which means a person made a mistake such as speeding, texting while driving or driving drunk. Self-driving cars will reduce the number of accidents caused by human error because they have many safety features like automatic emergency brakes (AEB). Some newer cars have advanced driver-assistance systems (ADAS) that help drivers. ADAS can warn the driver if the driver isn't paying attention.

Self-driving cars can drive for those who can't drive themselves and can also assist drivers to drive safely using ADAS.

Can self-driving cars assist people with disabilities and senior citizens?

In the United States, more than 20 million people have a disability. One of the greatest challenges for disabled people and senior citizens is transportation. Because of this, people who can't drive themselves are probably pretty excited about self-driving cars! Fully autonomous cars that don't need a human driver to steer, accelerate, brake, or do anything would benefit them the most. This is very important in cities where public transportation is limited or unavailable.

Self-driving cars can reduce traffic jams, improve road safety and save energy.

Can self-driving cars help reduce traffic jams? Self-driving cars can communicate with everything around them in the future. This is called "vehicle to everything" (V2X) communication. Being stuck in traffic is no fun. Self-driving cars can reduce traffic jams with the help of many sensor technologies, computer vision software, and V2X communication. Safety systems such as the front collision warning (FCW) system use radar sensors and camera technology to detect the distance to the vehicle in front and maintain a safe pace. Plus, self-driving cars can communicate with other self-driving cars and even smart traffic light systems to gather more information about the current traffic and what actions they should take. Reducing traffic jams and spending less time in the car is one of the other benefits of self-driving vehicles!

Self-driving cars can drive safely in school zones using sensors, cameras and computer vision software.

Are self-driving cars safe at busy school crossings? Safety at school crossings is important! You may have seen police officers helping students cross the road. The great thing about self-driving cars is that they will automatically follow the school zone speed limits and they will be able to see if small children are walking across the street. The cameras, computer vision software, and sensor technologies in self-driving cars help them to detect school signs, school zone speed limits, construction zones, other vehicles, small children, objects, and pedestrians. This is much safer than a normal distracted driver talking on the phone or wondering if they unplugged the toaster or brought their child's homework.

Self-driving cars can detect other cars near them using radars, cameras and assistive systems (ADAS).

Can self-driving cars drive at a safe distance? Many new cars have safety technologies such as the emergency automatic brakes (EAB), lane keep assist (LKA), lane departure warning (LDW), and adaptive cruise control (ACC), which help self-driving cars drive at a safe distance from neighboring cars. Adaptive cruise control means, the car's computer controls the speed. If a car gets too close to the car in front of it, the adaptive cruise control will slow the car down automatically by adjusting the speed. Radars and cameras help self-driving cars maintain a safe driving distance.

Self-driving cars must be able to perceive their environment under all weather conditions and unpredictable human behavior.

Do self-driving cars work in the rain? During bad weather, some of the sensors and cameras may not be able to see clearly, which is currently a challenge to enable self-driving cars. However, self-driving cars without a human driver, must be able to perceive the road better than human driver, make good decisions in the day or at night, in good weather and in dangerous weather such as heavy rain, fog, snow, dust, or high winds. Hundreds of research scientists and engineers all around the world are working hard to make sure self-driving cars will be safe no matter what. Did you know that if one sensor fails during bad weather, other sensors can act as a backup? These are called redundant sensors.

Self-driving cars rely on 3D maps of the roads with traffic lights, trees, buildings and other features.

What if there are no road signs? Self-driving cars use traffic lights, road signs, GPS, and other signals to figure out where they are and where they need to go. What about if there aren't any road signs? What if there aren't even any lanes? To be safe, these cars will have to learn to drive on narrow, steep, curvy roads, which may not have good road signs or maps. Scientists, engineers, car makers, and government policy makers, all have to work together to solve these challenges. As of 2019, fully autonomous cars that can drive through the mountains and remote areas without any help from a human driver are not available. But we can expect to see them in the roads soon.

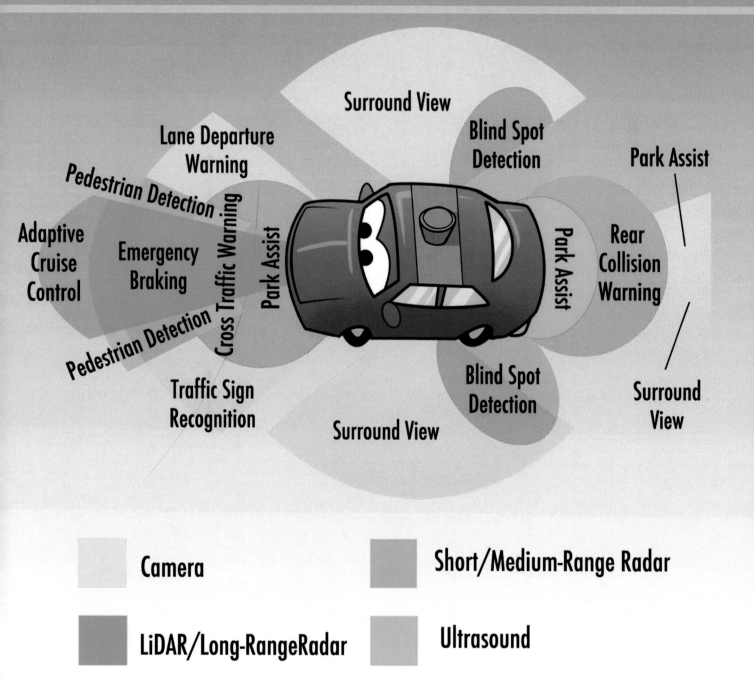

Surround View

Lane Departure Warning

Blind Spot Detection

Park Assist

Pedestrian Detection

Adaptive Cruise Control

Emergency Braking

Cross Traffic Warning

Park Assist

Park Assist

Rear Collision Warning

Pedestrian Detection

Traffic Sign Recognition

Blind Spot Detection

Surround View

Surround View

Camera

Short/Medium-Range Radar

LiDAR/Long-RangeRadar

Ultrasound

Can you tell which sensors help with the parking assistance?
Which sensor helps in blind spot detection?
Which sensor helps in surround view?

Can you point some of your favorite sensors in the picture?

Labels in image: LiDAR, GPS, Rear Camera, Radar, Ultrasonic Sensors, Odometry Sensors, Central Computer, Video Camera, Radar

Sensors in self-driving cars: We already use sensors in most cars. Know how the car beeps if your mom or dad doesn't buckle their seatbelt? It is due to a sensor! Self-driving cars have even more sensors and electronic equipment to make them safe. These safety features are enabled by many sensors such as cameras, ultrasonic sensors, GPS, radar, and LiDAR. High powered computers and software enable these sensors to work together so the car can drive safely by itself. Can you point some of your favorite sensors and the safety features in the picture?

Cameras: Did you know that there are multiple cameras in self-driving vehicles? These cameras can see on all sides of the car at the same time and collect data (images). With the help of computer vision software and artificial Intelligence, the data from the cameras and the sensors can be quickly analyzed so the car can identify objects, people, animals, obstacles, traffic lights and signs. The car then decides on the next course of action, which is, how to drive safely without hitting anyone! Cameras take hundreds of pictures per second and give self-driving cars superhuman vision.

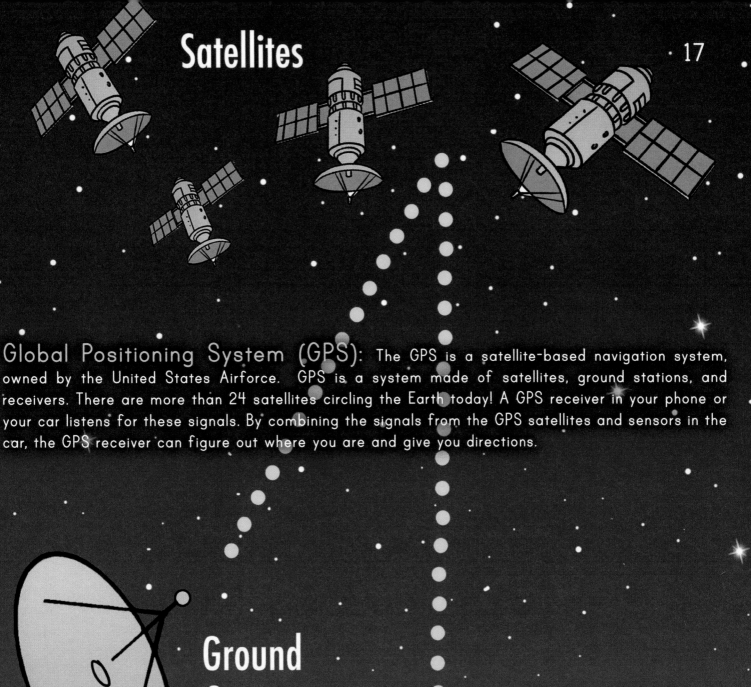

Satellites

Global Positioning System (GPS): The GPS is a satellite-based navigation system, owned by the United States Airforce. GPS is a system made of satellites, ground stations, and receivers. There are more than 24 satellites circling the Earth today! A GPS receiver in your phone or your car listens for these signals. By combining the signals from the GPS satellites and sensors in the car, the GPS receiver can figure out where you are and give you directions.

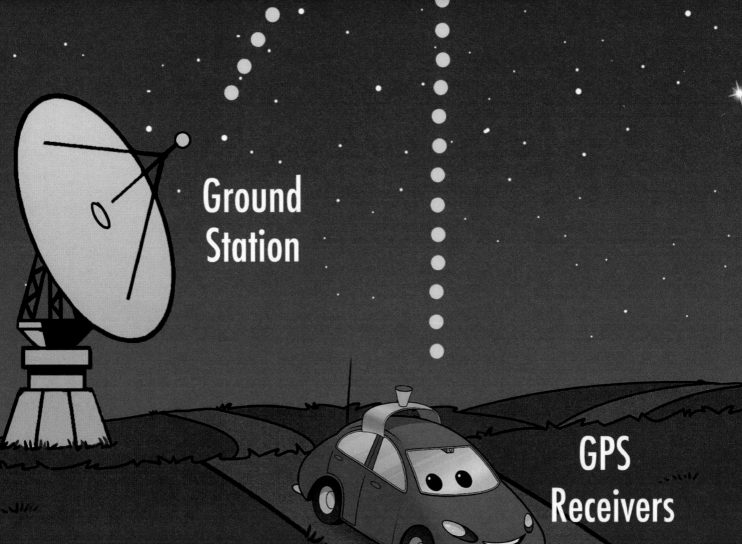

Ground Station

GPS Receivers

Ultrasonic Sensors: Remember how bats use echolocation to fly around at night? Self-driving cars have ultrasonic sensors that work the same way. The ultrasonic sensors send out sound waves and listen for an echo bouncing off of other objects on their path. However long the sound takes to come back tells the car how far away the other objects are. The sound wave frequencies that the ultrasonic sensors use are high enough that the human ear cannot hear them, but they are perfect for a car trying to park!

18

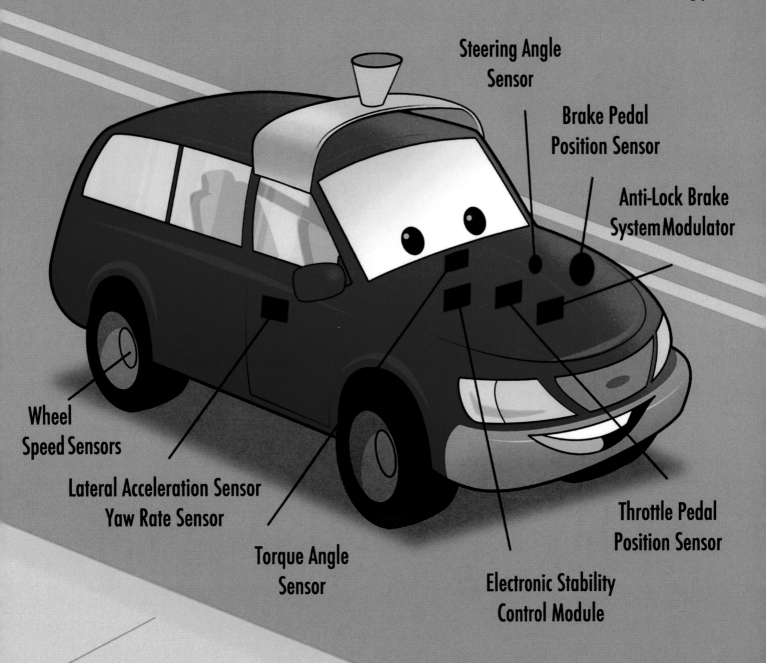

Steering Angle
Sensor

Brake Pedal
Position Sensor

Anti-Lock Brake
System Modulator

Wheel
Speed Sensors

Lateral Acceleration Sensor
Yaw Rate Sensor

Torque Angle
Sensor

Electronic Stability
Control Module

Throttle Pedal
Position Sensor

Wheel speed and angle sensors: The wheel speed sensor, also known as anti-lock brake sensor (ABS), records the rotational speed of the wheels and communicate this data to the engine control module (ECM). In addition to monitoring the speed, the wheel speed sensors are responsible for monitoring multiple vehicle functions such as traction control and anti-lock braking. Steering angle sensors determine where the front wheels are pointed. When combined with other data, it is possible to measure the dynamics of the vehicle. If the wheel sensors are covered with dirt or the wheel speed sensors are not working correctly, the warning light in the dashboard turns on. It is time to visit a car mechanic!

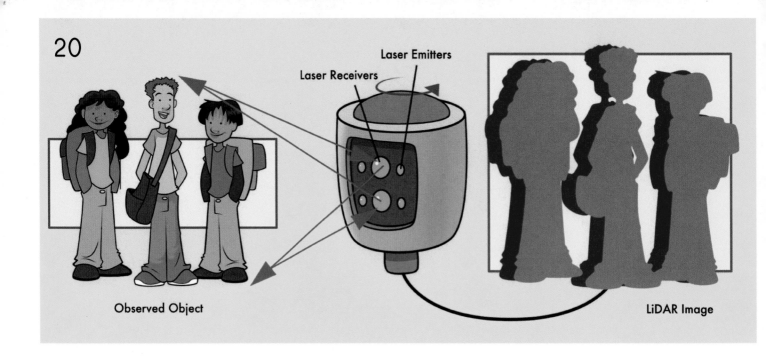

Laser Emitters

Laser Receivers

Observed Object

LiDAR Image

Light Detection and Ranging (LiDAR)

A LiDAR sensor shoots out laser lights pulses and measures distance by using the time it takes for those lights pulses to reflect back off of objects. The sensor does this in order to detect objects and their ranges. A "range" just means the distance to each part of an object. For example, LiDAR would measure the distance between a car and your nose, your cheeks, and your ears, not just "you." The LiDAR unit usually sits on top of the vehicle so it can create a 3D map of all sides of the car. Many lasers spin around the top of the car so fast that they can create a high-resolution 3D map of the surrounding environment in real time. Combined with the data from other sensors, the car's microprocessors can determine the identity and distance of any objects around the car. These sensors can also help find lane markings and the edges of the road.

Radio Detection and Ranging (Radar)

Radar is the heart of the self-driving cars and the ADAS. Safety features such as adaptive cruise control, automatic braking, park assist, blind spot detection, lane assist and cross-traffic alert, take advantage of radar technology. Radar is often located in the front bumper of the self-driving car and use radio wave or micro-wave in the electromagnetic spectrum (EMS), to detect objects, relative speed and the distance from the car. Depending on the type, short range, medium range and long-range radar, radar can work more than 100 meters away – longer than a football field! Radar sends high frequency radio waves into the air, and those waves bounce off objects and back to the car. In many cars, radar sensors are used to alert the driver when objects are detected in the car's blind spot. Compared to LiDAR, radar may be less affected by weather conditions such as rain, fog, wind, darkness, or bright sun. Maybe you've heard of radar before. Police officers use radar guns to catch speeding cars. Radar can measure the speed of an object due to something called the Doppler effect.

High definition mapping

What do self-driving systems do with all this information from the sensors and the GPS? They create and maintain an internal map of their surroundings. The map has to be perfect, which is why there are so many sensors and cameras in self-driving cars. The car's software and computers use the map to plot a safe path for the car, and then sends instructions to the vehicle's actuators which control speed, brakes, and steering. All the sensors, software, hardware and the micro-processors must work together to make self-driving cars a reality!

Self-driving cars are here. They are
going to change the world in a big way!

Are you ready?

Learning Assessment

1. Can you list some of the benefits of self-driving cars?

2. Can you list some challenges for self-driving cars?

3. Innovate!

Self-driving cars are here. They are going to change the world in a big way! Based on some of the benefits and challenges you have learned about, take a piece of paper and draw a picture of your own design for a self-driving car or vehicle. Be creative, and remember to label the parts and include some sensors.

4. Mix and Match!

Based on what you have learnt, can you match the two columns?

Camera   Park assist

Ultrasonic sensors   Laser pulses for distance sensing

LiDAR   Blind spot detection

Radar   360-degree surround view vision

Would you like to read more about
self-driving cars, sensors, robotics, drones, AI and other exciting STEM fields?
Check out our other books coming soon at
https://just-empower.com

Glossary

Self-driving car: A self-driving vehicle is capable of driving itself and doesn't need a human driver. There are many levels of driving automation. The Society of Automotive Engineers (www.sae.org) defines 6 levels of driving automation ranging from level 0 (fully manual) to level 5 (fully autonomous). Autonomous vehicles are typically classified at levels 3, 4, or 5 for driving automation.

Obstacle: Something that stands in your way or blocks your way.

INS: An Inertial Navigation System is a device that uses many sensors such as motion sensors and rotation sensors to calculate the position, direction, and speed of a moving object.

Computer vision: The systems that are responsible for an autonomous vehicle's ability to "see" its environment. Examples are the Artificial Intelligence (AI) software and microprocessors that can help process data from the sensors, label and recognize objects and patterns.

NHTSA: The National Highway Traffic Safety Administration is an agency of the U.S. federal government, part of the Department of Transportation.

Human error: According to Merriam-Webster, human error is a person's mistake as opposed to the failure of a machine.

ADAS: An Advanced Driver Assistance System is a vehicle system designed to improve driving safety; it includes things like adaptive cruise control and lane departure warning.

AI: Artificial Intelligence is the ability of a machine to "think" and make decisions almost like a person would.

Doppler effect: According to Britannica, the apparent difference between the frequency at which sound or light waves leave a source and that at which they reach an observer, caused by relative motion of the observer and the wave source.

Electromagnetic spectrum: According to Britannica, the entire range of wavelengths or frequencies of electromagnetic radiation extending from gamma rays to the radio waves including visible light.

References

https://www.sae.org/automated-unmanned-vehicles/

https://www.nhtsa.gov/

https://crashstats.nhtsa.dot.gov/Api/Public/ViewPublication/812115

https://www.who.int/news-room/fact-sheets/detail/road-traffic-injuries

https://www.who.int/disabilities/world_report/2011/report/en/

https://www.nhtsa.gov/press-releases/10-automakers-equipped-most-their-2018-vehicles-automatic-emergency-braking

https://www.gps.gov/multimedia/images/constellation.jpg

https://www.britannica.com/science/Doppler-effect

https://www.britannica.com/science/electromagnetic-spectrum

Draw, color and label a picture of your own
design for self-driving cars, trucks or vehicles.

Be creative and remember to label the
parts and include some sensors.

Draw, color and label a picture of your own
design for self-driving cars, trucks or vehicles.

Be creative and remember to label the
parts and include some sensors.

About the authors, Anna Prakash-Ashton & Elaina Ashton:

We are a mother-daughter team based in Chandler, Arizona, USA. We love technology and giving back to the community. We co-founded our non-profit organization, Education Empowers Inc., (www.educationempowers.org), to share our passion for STEM (Science, Technology, Engineering, Math), robotics, and sustainability education. As of Spring 2020, our curriculum and STEM-robotics clubs are in more than 50 locations in Arizona, USA and growing globally.

Anna Prakash-Ashton is an engineer by profession and the winner of the prestigious Society of Women Engineers (SWE) "Prism" award in 2017, for her contributions to technology and STEM advocacy for girls, young women, the underrepresented, and the underserved children. Anna has several technical publications and patents covering sensors, displays, optoelectronics, and semiconductor packaging materials & processes.

Elaina Ashton is currently a high school senior in Chandler, Arizona, and the president of her high school robotics club. She is the winner of the Cox Connect2STEM award, Junior achievement of Arizona's 18 Under 18 award, and the SWEnext – Local Innovator award.

We sincerely hope that this material and our other books in this series, can help you to start a STEM-robotics club or a maker club in your local community or school. Well... what are you waiting for?

Made in the USA
Monee, IL
15 September 2020